RHYTHMS AND BE[YOND]

21 Lessons in Rhythm Skill Development for All [Musicians]

BY TIMOTHY LOEST
AND TIMOTHY WIMER

Table of Contents

Production: Frank and Gail Hackinson
Production Coordinator: Philip Groeber
Editors: Deborah A. Sheldon and Margene Pappas
Cover & Illustrations: Terpstra Design, San Francisco
Text Design: K.B. Dalzell
Engraving: Tempo Music Press, Inc.
Printer: Tempo Music Press, Inc.

ISBN-13: 978-1-56939-683-4

2

Lesson 1
Whole, Half, and Quarter Notes

$\frac{4}{4}$ Time

The lessons in this book begin in $\frac{4}{4}$ time. There are four beats per measure in $\frac{4}{4}$ time, and the quarter note receives one beat. $\frac{4}{4}$ time is sometimes referred to as common time. $\frac{4}{4}$ or common time is indicated by two time signatures, $\frac{4}{4}$ or **C**.

Whole Note

The whole note receives four beats in $\frac{4}{4}$ time. The whole note's attack begins on beat one and its sound continues through beat four.

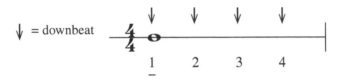

Note: In this book, underlined counts represent the attack or entry point of each note.

Half Note

The half note receives two beats in $\frac{4}{4}$ time. When there are two half notes in a measure, the first half note's attack begins on beat one and its sound continues through beat two. The second half note's attack begins on beat three and its sound continues through beat four.

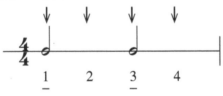

Quarter Note

The quarter note receives one beat in $\frac{4}{4}$ time. When there are four quarter notes in a measure, each beat is played.

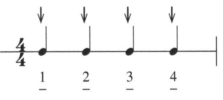

Lesson 1 Exercises

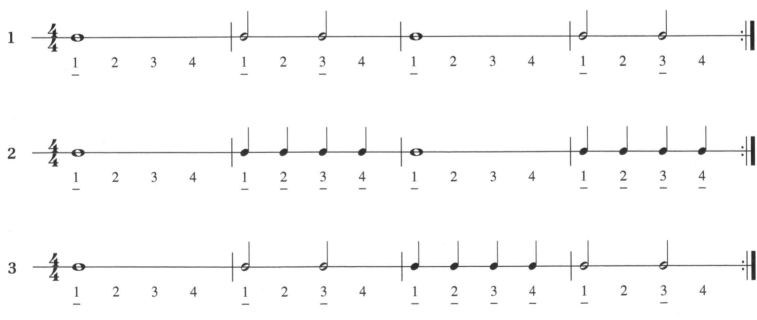

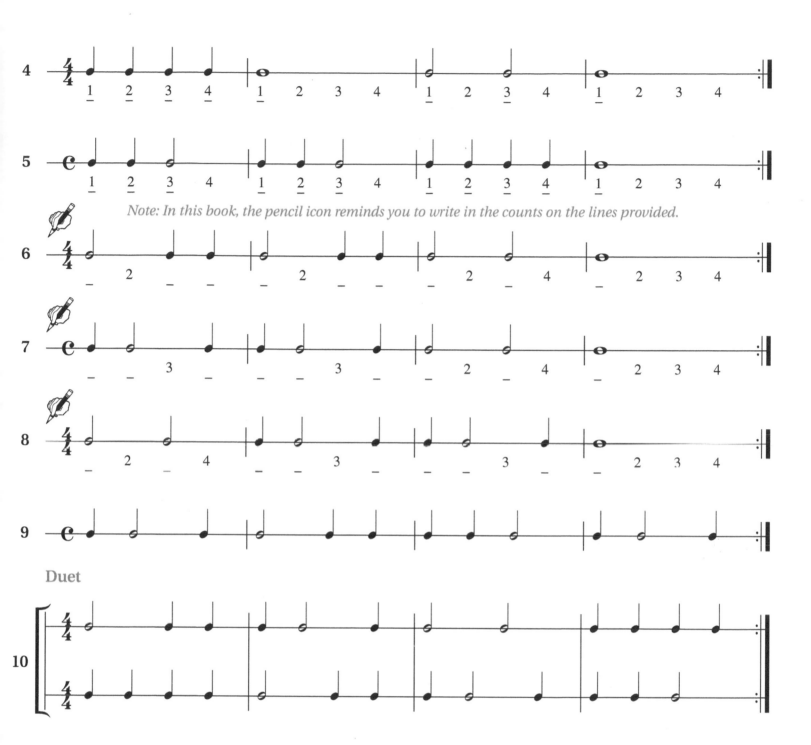

Note: In this book, the pencil icon reminds you to write in the counts on the lines provided.

Duet

MYSTERY RHYTHM

The following rhythm is from a familiar folk song about a girl and her pet. Play the rhythm and see if you can identify the melody. Once you solve the mystery, choose a starting pitch and try to play the melody by ear.

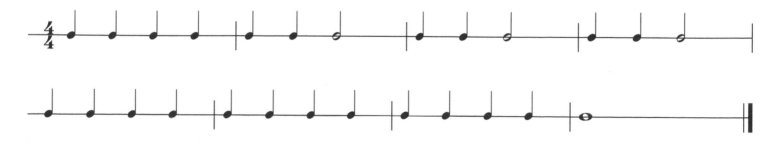

Lesson 2
Whole, Half, and Quarter Rests

Whole Rest

The whole rest receives four beats in $\frac{4}{4}$ time. When a measure contains a whole rest, no sound is made for four beats. The whole rest looks like an *upside down top hat.*

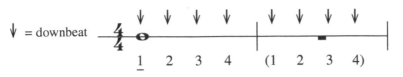

Note: In this book, rest counts appear in parenthesis.

Half Rest

The half rest receives two beats in $\frac{4}{4}$ time. When a measure contains a half rest, no sound is made for two beats. The half rest looks like a *top hat.*

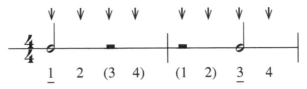

Quarter Rest

The quarter rest receives one beat in $\frac{4}{4}$ time. When a measure contains a quarter rest, no sound is made for one beat. The quarter rest looks like a *lightning bolt.*

Lesson 1 Exercises

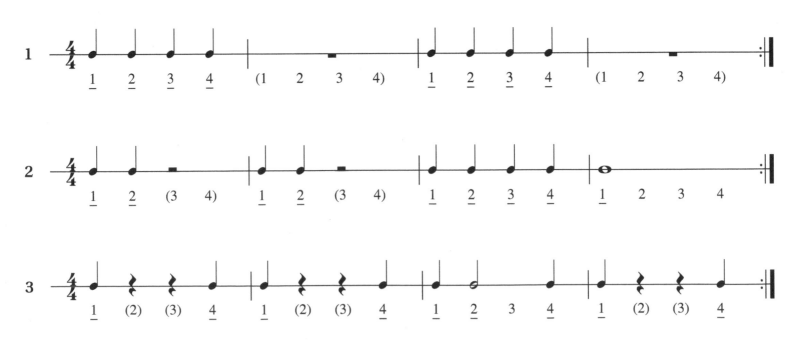

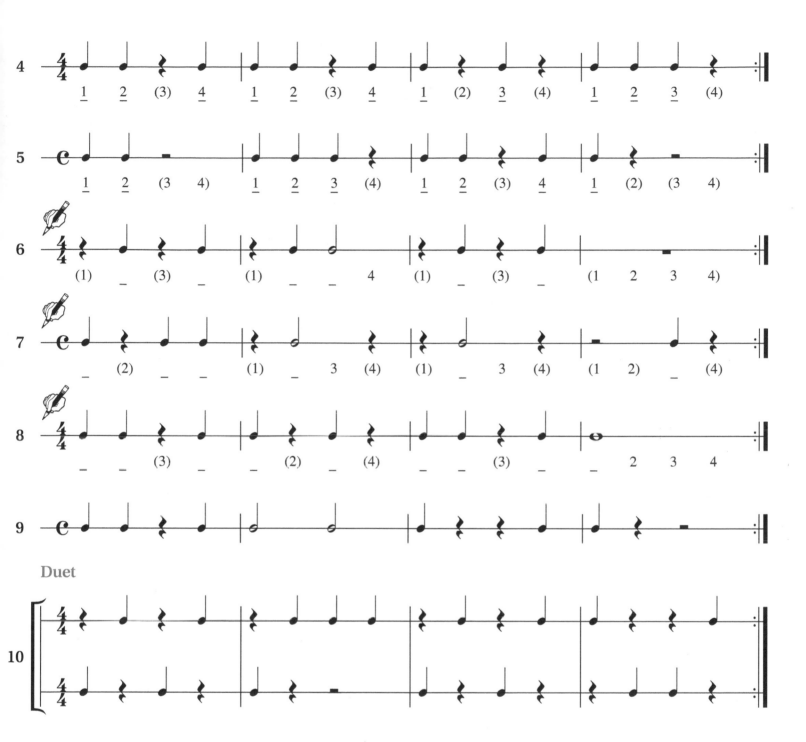

Duet

MYSTERY RHYTHM

The following rhythm is from a familiar English folk song about pastry. Play the rhythm and see if you can identify the melody. Once you solve mystery, choose a starting pitch and try to play the melody by ear.

Tip: Try playing this Mystery Rhythm at a fast tempo.

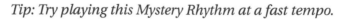

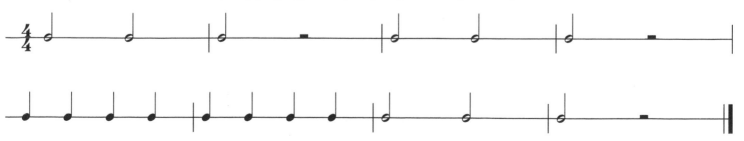

Lesson 3
Eighth Notes

Eighth Note

The eighth note receives one-half beat in $\frac{4}{4}$ time, so eight of them can fit into each measure. Individual eighth notes have flags attached to their stems.

Repeated Eighth Notes

Repeated eighth notes are beamed together in groups of two or four. The notes with upward arrows are known as upbeats. Each upbeat is marked "+" and is counted "and."

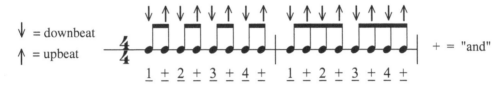

Eighth-Note Subdivision

When a measure or phrase contains eighth notes, it is helpful to think downbeat and upbeat counts for each beat. This counting technique is called eighth-note subdivision. When subdividing, remember that each beat contains a built-in "+" count.

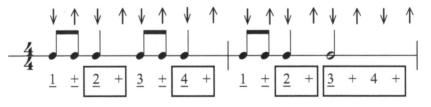

Note: In the above example, subdivided counts appear in boxes.

Lesson 3 Exercises

Tip: Think eighth-note subdivision.

RHYTHM REVIEW

Match each note and rest with its correct definition in $\frac{4}{4}$ time.

1. _____ a note that gets one beat
2. _____ a rest that gets four beats
3. _____ a rest that gets one beat
4. _____ a note that gets four beats
5. _____ a rest that gets two beats
6. _____ a note that gets one-half beat
7. _____ a note that gets two beats

A. whole note **o**
B. half note ♩
C. quarter note ♩
D. eighth note ♪
E. whole rest ▬
F. half rest ▬
G. quarter rest 𝄽

Lesson 4
Eighth Rests

Eighth Rest

The eighth rest receives one-half beat in $\frac{4}{4}$ time, so eight of them can fit into each measure.

↓ = downbeat
↑ = upbeat

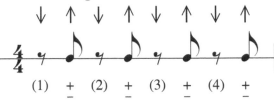

(1) (+) (2) (+) (3) (+) (4) (+)

Eighth Rests on Downbeats

Eighth rests can replace downbeat eighth notes.

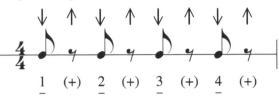

(1) + (2) + (3) + (4) +

Eighth Rests on Upbeats

Eighth rests can replace upbeat eighth notes.

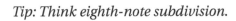

1 (+) 2 (+) 3 (+) 4 (+)

Lesson 4 Exercises

Tip: Think eighth-note subdivision.

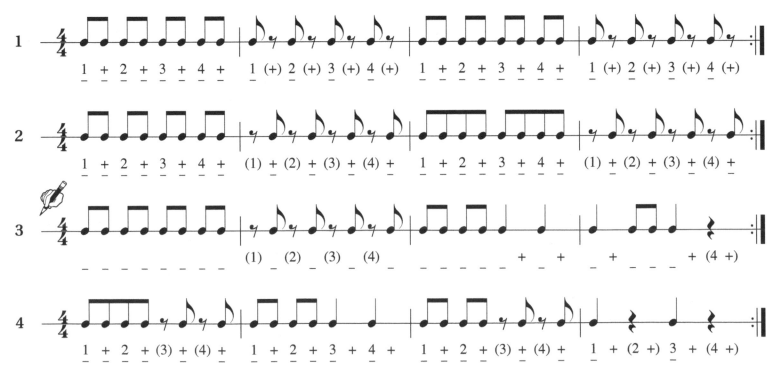

MUSIC MATH

Add up the note and rest values in each column.

Answer: 4

Lesson 5
Tied Notes

Tie

A tie combines the value of two or more notes. Attack only the first note in a tie.

Lesson 5 Exercises

Tip: It is not necessary to think eighth-note subdivision for exercises 1–5.

Tip: Think eighth-note subdivision for exercises 6–10.

Lesson 6
Dotted Half Notes

Dotted Half Note

A dot following a note increases the note's value by one-half. Because a half note receives two beats in $\frac{4}{4}$ time, a dotted half note is equal to three beats or three tied quarter notes.

Lesson 5 Exercises

Tip: It is not necessary to think eighth-note subdivision for exercises 1–5.

Tip: Think eighth-note subdivision for exercises 6–10. Eighth-note subdivision also applies to dotted half notes.

Lesson 7
Dotted Quarter Notes

Dotted Quarter Note

A dot following a note increases the note's value by one-half. Because a quarter note receives one beat in $\frac{4}{4}$ time, a dotted quarter note is equal to one and one-half beats or three tied eighth notes.

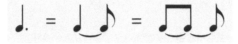

Dotted Quarter Note / Eighth Note Rhythm

A dotted quarter note is usually followed by an eighth note. The combined value of both notes equals two beats.

Eighth Note / Dotted Quarter Note Rhythm

Occasionally, an eighth note may precede a dotted quarter note. The combined value of both notes equals two beats.

Lesson 7 Exercises

Tip: Think eighth-note subdivision. Eighth-note subdivision also applies to dotted quarter notes.

Duet

MYSTERY RHYTHM

The following rhythm is from a famous Beethoven symphony. Play the rhythm and see if you can identify the melody. Once you solve the mystery, choose a starting pitch and try to play the melody by ear.

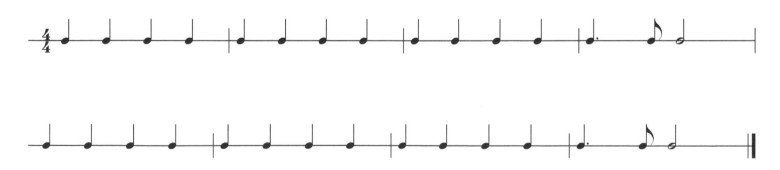

Lesson 8
Syncopation

Syncopation

Syncopation occurs when a weak beat is accented. In addition, the syncopated note is held or tied to a strong beat.

Eighth Note / Quarter Note / Eighth Note Syncopation

The most common syncopation is the eighth note / quarter note / eighth note syncopation. Notice that the syncopation occurs on an upbeat that is accented.

Lesson 8 Exercises

Tip: It is not necessary to think eighth-note subdivision for exercises 1–3.

Tip: Think eighth-note subdivision for exercises 4–10.
Eighth-note subdivision especially applies to syncopated quarter notes.

Lesson 9
Sixteenth Notes

Sixteenth Note

The sixteenth note receives one-fourth beat in $\frac{4}{4}$ time, so sixteen of them can fit into each measure. Individual sixteenth notes have double flags attached to their stems.

Repeated Sixteenth Notes

Repeated sixteenth notes come in groups of four and are connected with a double beam. They are counted "1 e + a   2 e + a   3 e + a   4 e + a."

↓ = downbeat
↑ = upbeat

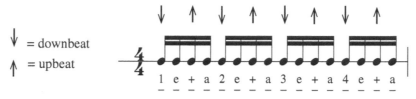

Note Value Chart

A quarter note has the same value as two tied eighth notes or four tied sixteenth notes.

quarter note = 1 beat each

eighth note = 1/2 beat each

sixteenth note = 1/4 beat each

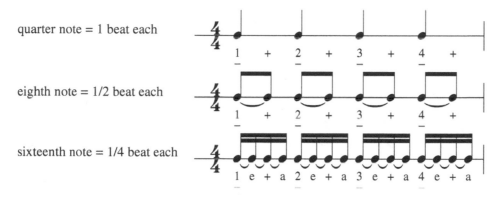

Lesson 9 Exercises

Tip: Think eighth-note subdivision for notes and rests receiving one or more beats.

16

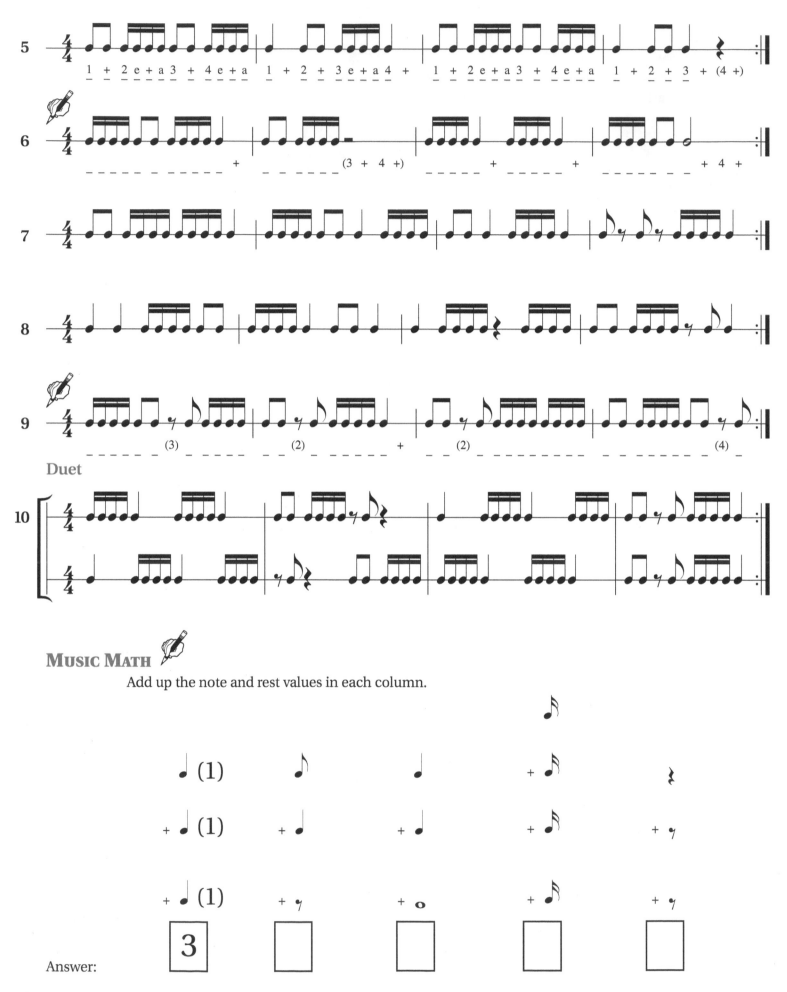

MUSIC MATH

Add up the note and rest values in each column.

Answer: 3

BB207

Lesson 10
Eighth Note / Two Sixteenth Note Group

Eighth Note / Two Sixteenth Note Group

An eighth note can replace the first two sixteenth notes in a group of four sixteenth notes. This creates an eighth note / two sixteenth note group.

Eighth Rest / Two Sixteenth Note Group

An eighth rest can replace the eighth note to create an eighth rest / two sixteenth note group.

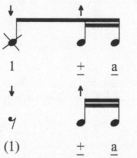

Lesson 10 Exercises

Tip: Think eighth-note subdivision for notes and rests receiving one or more beats.

Lesson 11
Two Sixteenth Note / Eighth Note Group

Two Sixteenth Note / Eighth Note Group

An eighth note can replace the last two sixteenth notes in a group of four sixteenth notes. This creates a two sixteenth note / eighth note group.

Two Sixteenth Note / Eighth Rest Group

An eighth rest can replace the eighth note to create a two sixteenth note / eighth rest group.

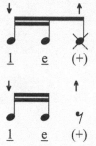

Lesson 11 Exercises

Tip: Think eighth-note subdivision for notes and rests receiving one or more beats.

20

BB207

Lesson 12
Sixteenth Note / Eighth Note / Sixteenth Note Group

Sixteenth Note / Eighth Note / Sixteenth Note Group

An eighth note can replace the middle two sixteenth notes in a group of four sixteenth notes. This creates a sixteenth note / eighth note / sixteenth note group.

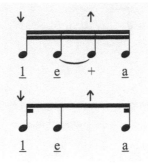

Lesson 12 Exercises

Tip: Think eighth-note subdivision for notes and rests receiving one or more beats.

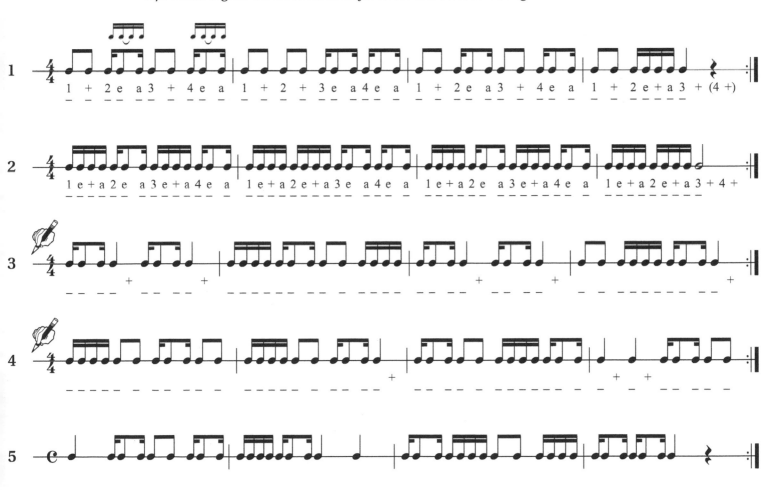

BAFFLING BARLINES

Separate the notes and rests into measures by drawing barlines in the correct places.
The first measure of each line has been started for you.

Tip: This is a horizontal Music Math activity!

Lesson 13
Dotted Eighth Note / Sixteenth Note Group

Dotted Eighth Note

A dot following a note increases the note's value by one-half. Because an eighth note receives one-half beat in $\frac{4}{4}$ time, a dotted eighth note is equal to three-fourths of a beat or three tied sixteenth notes.

Dotted Eighth Note / Sixteenth Note Group

A dotted eighth note can replace the first three sixteenth notes in a group of four sixteenth notes. This creates a dotted eighth note / sixteenth note group.

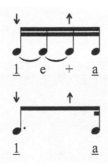

Lesson 13 Exercises

Tip: Think eighth-note subdivision for notes and rests receiving one or more beats.

24

BAFFLING BARLINES

Separate the notes and rests into measures by drawing barlines in the correct places.
The first measure of each line has been started for you.

Tip: This is a horizontal Music Math activity!

Lesson 14
Sixteenth Rests

Sixteenth Rest

The sixteenth rest receives one-fourth beat in $\frac{4}{4}$ time, so sixteen of them can fit into each measure.

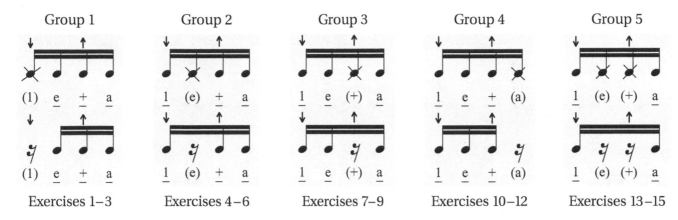

↓ = downbeat
↑ = upbeat

(1)(e)(+)(a)(2)(e)(+)(a)(3)(e)(+)(a)(4)(e)(+)(a)

Sixteenth Note / Sixteenth Rest Groups

A sixteenth rest can replace any sixteenth note in a group of four to create a variety of six-teenth note / sixteenth rest groups.

Group 1	Group 2	Group 3	Group 4	Group 5
Exercises 1–3	Exercises 4–6	Exercises 7–9	Exercises 10–12	Exercises 13–15

Lesson 14 Exercises

Tip: Think eighth-note subdivision for notes and rests receiving one or more beats.

Group 1

Group 2

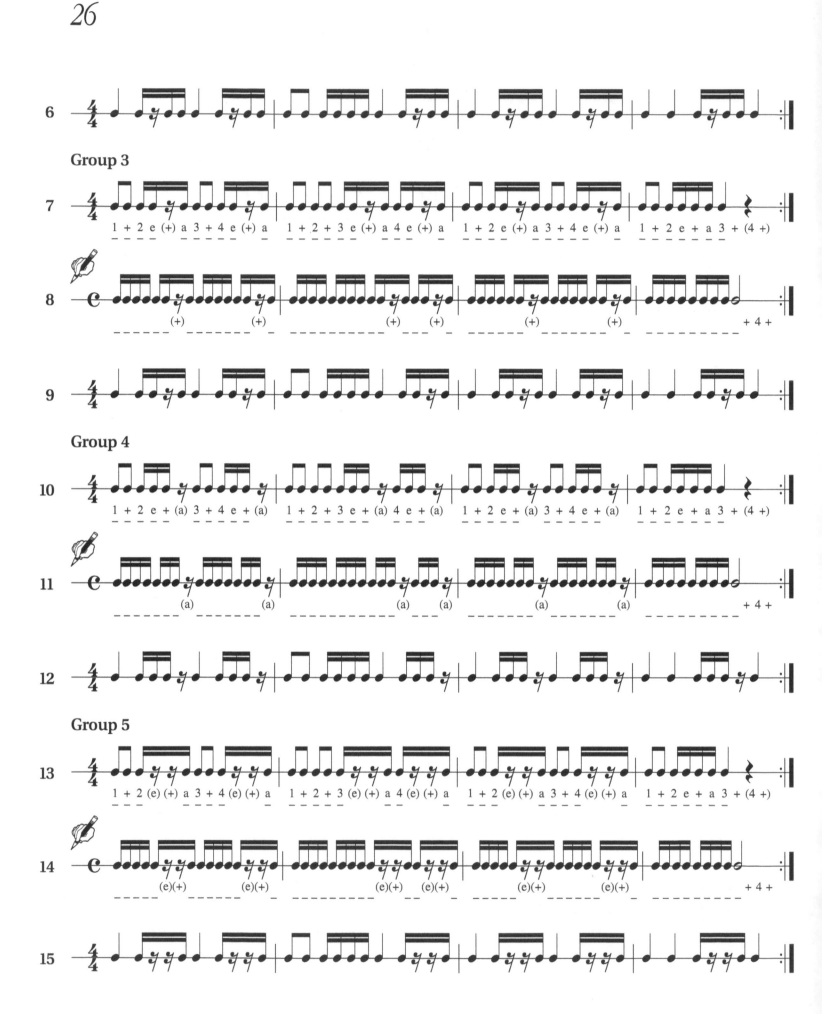

Lesson 15
Triplets

Triplet

A triplet is a group of three notes played evenly in the space of two similar notes. Triplets are identified by the numeral "3" located above each triplet grouping.

Eighth Note Triplet

An eighth note triplet consists of three notes connected with a single beam. Because an eighth note triplet takes up one beat in $\frac{4}{4}$ time, four eighth note triplets can fit into each measure. There are many different ways to count eighth note triplets. We suggest "1 is a   2 is a   3 is a   4 is a."

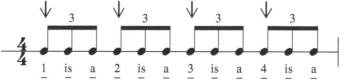

Sixteenth Note Triplet

A sixteenth note triplet consists of three sixteenth notes connected with a double beam. Because a sixteenth note triplet takes up one-half beat in $\frac{4}{4}$ time, eight sixteenth note triplets can fit into each measure.

Sixteenth Note Sextuplet

Two neighboring sixteenth note triplets are usually notated together to form a sixteenth note sextuplet. Because each sextuplet takes up one beat in $\frac{4}{4}$ time, four sextuplets can fit into each measure. Sextuplets are counted "1 is a + is a   2 is a + is a   3 is a + is a   4 is a + is a."

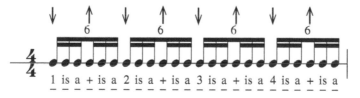

Eighth Note / Sixteenth Note Triplet Group

An eighth note can be combined with a sixteenth note triplet to create an eighth note / sixteenth note triplet group.

Sixteenth Note Triplet / Eighth Note Group

A sixteenth note triplet can be combined with an eighth note to create a sixteenth note triplet / eighth note group.

Quarter Note Triplet

A quarter note triplet consists of three quarter notes. Because a quarter note triplet takes up two beats in $\frac{4}{4}$ time, two quarter note triplets can fit into each measure. Quarter note triplets have an evenly spaced feel. We suggest counting them "1 is a   3 is a."

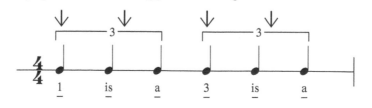

Lesson 15 Exercises   *Tip: Think eighth-note subdivision for notes and rests receiving one or more beats.*

Sixteenth Note Sextuplets   *Tip: Exercises 7–14 should first be played at a slow tempo.*

Eighth Note / Sixteenth Note Triplet Group

Lesson 16
2/4 Time

2/4 Time

There are two beats per measure in 2/4 time. The quarter note receives one beat and the half note receives two beats.

Lesson 16 Exercises

Tip: Think eighth-note subdivision for notes and rests receiving one or more beats.

Lesson 17
¾ Time

¾ Time

There are three beats per measure in ¾ time. The quarter note receives one beat, the half note receives two beats, and the dotted half note receives three beats.

Lesson 17 Exercises

Tip: Think eighth-note subdivision for notes and rests receiving one or more beats.

Lesson 18
Cut Time (Alla Breve)

Cut Time (Alla Breve) Time Signatures

Cut time is indicated by two time signatures, ₵ or 𝟤/𝟤.

Note and Rest Values in Cut Time

In cut time, note and rest values are cut in half, giving the tempo a "double-time" feel.

o or — in ₵ = 2 beats	♩ or 𝄾 in ₵ = 1/2 beat
♩ or — in ₵ = 1 beat	♪ or ♪ in ₵ = 1/4 beat

Lesson 18 Exercises

*Tip: Although note and rest values are cut in half in cut time,
you should continue to subdivide each beat.*

*Note: Exercises 1, 4, 7, 10, and 13 have been notated twice to show
the relationship between cut time and 𝟤/𝟦 time.*

RHYTHM REVIEW

Match each note and rest with its correct definition in $\frac{2}{2}$ time.

1. _____ a note that gets one beat
2. _____ a rest that gets two beats
3. _____ a rest that gets one beat
4. _____ a rest that gets one-half beat
5. _____ a note that gets two beats
6. _____ a note that gets one-half beat
7. _____ a rest that gets one-fourth beat
8. _____ a note that gets one-fourth beat

A. whole note
B. half note
C. quarter note
D. eighth note
E. whole rest
F. half rest
G. quarter rest
H. eighth rest

For More Practice

Return to Lesson 1 and try counting, clapping, and playing each exercise in cut time.
Once you have mastered Lesson 1, try Lessons 2–4 in cut time.

Lesson 19
Cut Time Syncopation

Syncopation Review

Syncopation occurs when a weak beat is accented. In addition, the syncopated note is held or tied to a strong beat.

Quarter Note / Half Note / Quarter Note Syncopation

The most common syncopation in cut time is the quarter note / half note / quarter note syncopation. Compare this rhythm to the eighth note / quarter note / eighth note syncopation found on page 14. In both instances, the syncopation occurs on an upbeat that is accented.

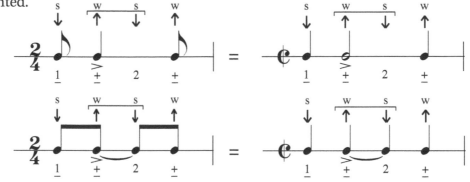

Lesson 19 Exercises

Tip: Continue to subdivide each beat.

Note: Exercises 1, 3, and 5 have been notated twice to show the relationship between cut time and $\frac{2}{4}$ time.

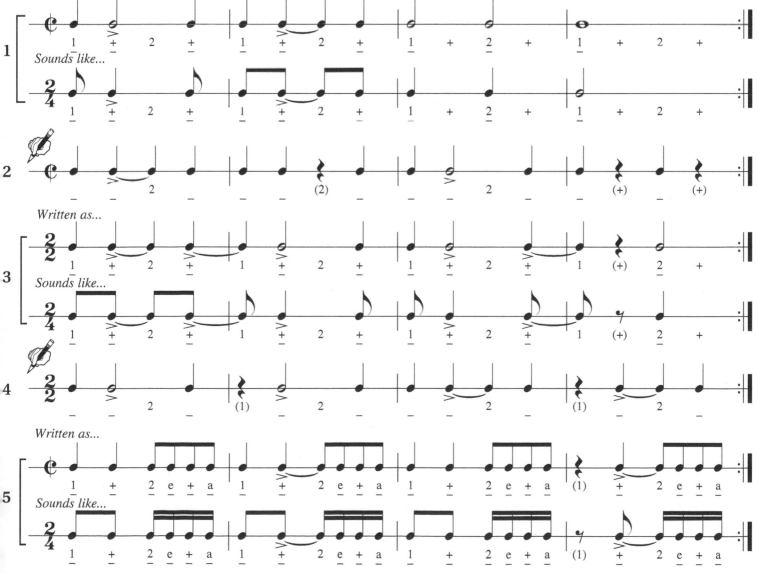

Lesson 20
Slow $\frac{6}{8}$ Time (in six)

Slow $\frac{6}{8}$ Time (in six)

There are six beats per measure in slow $\frac{6}{8}$ time and the eighth note receives one beat.

Note and Rest Values in Slow $\frac{6}{8}$ Time

There are four common note and rest values in slow $\frac{6}{8}$ time.

$\stackrel{}{\partial}\cdot$ or $\rule{0.4cm}{0.08cm}\cdot$ in $\frac{6}{8}$ time = 6 beats $\rule{}{} \downarrow$ or ξ in $\frac{6}{8}$ time = 2 beats

$\downarrow\cdot$ or $\xi\cdot$ in $\frac{6}{8}$ time = 3 beats $\downarrow$ or γ in $\frac{6}{8}$ time = 1 beat

Lesson 20 Exercises

Tip: Think eighth–note subdivision for quarter, dotted quarter, and half notes and rests.
In slow $\frac{6}{8}$ time, however, the eighth note receives one beat.

MYSTERY RHYTHM

The following rhythm is from an old English folk song. Play the rhythm and see if you can identify the melody. Once you solve the mystery, choose a starting pitch and try to play the melody by ear.

Note: This rhythm begins with a pickup eighth note located on beat six.

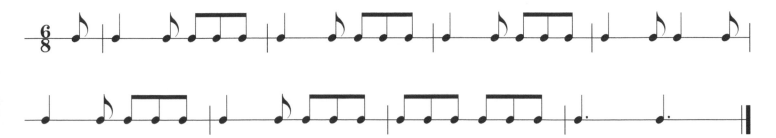

Lesson 21
Fast $\frac{6}{8}$ Time (in two)

Fast $\frac{6}{8}$ Time (in two)

In fast $\frac{6}{8}$ time, each measure consists of six eighth notes. Unlike slow $\frac{6}{8}$ time, fast $\frac{6}{8}$ time is played with a "two-beat" feel. Because six eighth notes must be spread evenly across two beats, each beat will consist of three beamed eighth notes. There are many ways to count eighth notes in fast $\frac{6}{8}$ time. We suggest "1 is a   2 is a."

Note and Rest Values in Fast $\frac{6}{8}$ Time

In fast $\frac{6}{8}$ time, the eighth note receives one-third beat. There are four common note and rest values in fast $\frac{6}{8}$ time.

$\cdot$ or $\blacksquare$• in fast $\frac{6}{8}$ time = 2 beats

$\cdot$ or $\} $ in fast $\frac{6}{8}$ time = 2/3 beat

$\cdot$ or $\}\cdot$ in fast $\frac{6}{8}$ time = 1 beat

$\cdot$ or γ in fast $\frac{6}{8}$ time = 1/3 beat

Common Rhythmic Segments in Fast $\frac{6}{8}$ Time

There are five common rhythmic segments in fast $\frac{6}{8}$ time. Segments 1, 2, 4, and 5 can be combined to create one-measure rhythmic units.

Lesson 21 Exercises

Tip: Think eighth–note subdivision for quarter, dotted quarter, and dotted half notes and rests. In fast $\frac{6}{8}$ time, the eighth note receives one-third beat.

Bonus Tip: Look for each rhythmic segment as you play.

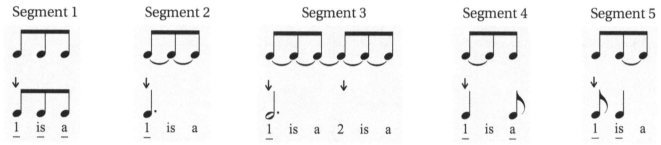

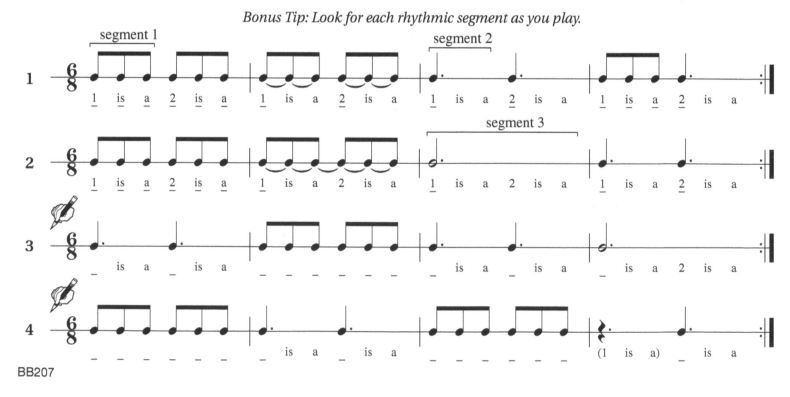

Special Activity Answer Key

Lesson 1 – Page 3
MYSTERY RHYTHM: *Mary Had a Little Lamb*

Lesson 2 – Page 5
MYSTERY RHYTHM: *Hot Cross Buns*

Lesson 3 – Page 7
RHYTHM REVIEW: 1) C   2) E   3) G   4) A   5) F   6) D   7) B

Lesson 4 – Page 9
MUSIC MATH: 4   3   3   4   4

Lesson 7 – Page 13
MYSTERY RHYTHM: *Symphony No. 9, "Ode to Joy"*

Lesson 9 – Page 16
MUSIC MATH: 3   2   6   1   2

Lesson 12 – Page 22
BAFFLING BARLINES:

Lesson 13 – Page 24
BAFFLING BARLINES:

Lesson 18 – Page 34
RHYTHM REVIEW: 1) B   2) E   3) F   4) G   5) A   6) C   7) H   8) D

Lesson 20 – Page 37
MYSTERY RHYTHM: *Greensleeves*